BRITISH HISTORY MAKERS

Boudicca

Claire Throp

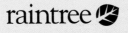

raintree

a Capstone company — publishers for children

Raintree is an imprint of Capstone Global Library Limited, a company incorporated in England and Wales having its registered office at 264 Banbury Road, Oxford, OX2 7DY – Registered company number: 6695582

www.raintree.co.uk
myorders@raintree.co.uk

Edited by Linda Staniford
Designed by Steve Mead
Original illustrations © Capstone Global Library Limited 2017
Illustrated by Martin Sanders (Beehive Illustration)
Picture research by Ruth Smith
Production by Tori Abraham
Originated by Capstone Global Library
Printed and bound in China

ISBN 978 1 474 73408 0
20 19 18 17 16
10 9 8 7 6 5 4 3 2 1

British Library Cataloguing in Publication Data
A full catalogue record for this book is available from the British Library.

Acknowledgements
We would like to thank the following for permission to reproduce photographs:
Alamy: Lebrecht Music and Arts Photo Library, 5, Pete Davis, 8, Philip Sharp, 16, Richard Iestyn Hughes, 15; Capstone Press: cover, 7, 23; Dreamstime: Rogerashford, 19; Getty Images: Hulton Archive, 21, Popperfoto, 22, Heritage Images, 18, 20; Mary Evans Picture Library: cover; © Robert Edwards: 27

Shutterstock: abxyz, 11, Aleks Melnik, cover, title page, Antony McAulay, 13, Claudio Divizia, 26, Jule_Berlin, 17, lynea, 14, Natalyon, cover, background design elements, Philip Bird LRPS CPAGB, 4, Renata Sedmakova, 9, Romas_Photo, 24, Toluk, cover, background design elements; Thinkstock: PHOTOS.com, 25; Wikimedia: Ad Meskens, 12, PHGCOM, 6

We would like to thank Dr Mark Zumbuhl of the University of Oxford for his invaluable help in the preparation of this book.

Every effort has been made to contact copyright holders of material reproduced in this book. Any omissions will be rectified in subsequent printings if notice is given to the publisher.

Some words are shown in bold, **like this**. You can find out what they mean by looking in the glossary.

Contents

Boudicca's life

Boudicca is famous for leading a major **rebellion** against the **Romans** in the 1st century AD. The fact that she was a woman made it even more impressive. It was rare for a woman to lead at that time.

Boudicca was "very tall", had a "harsh" voice and appeared "most terrifying" wrote a Roman called Cassius Dio. However, we don't know where he got this information from or how true it is.

Tribal life

In the 1st century AD, the people of Britain lived in groups called **tribes**. Boudicca belonged to the Iceni tribe. The Iceni lived in what is now Norfolk and north Suffolk. Most were farmers, but some did metalwork or made pottery.

⌘ FACT ⌘

Horses were important for the Iceni. They were symbols of wealth and power. Many Iceni coins have pictures of horses on them.

This map shows where the tribes lived in Boudicca's time.

N
W E
S

Atlantic Ocean

North Sea

CALEDONI

VACOMAGI

TAEXALI

VENICONES

DUMNONII

SELGOVAE

VOTADINI

NOVANTAE

BRICANTES

PARISI

DECANGI

CONELTAUVI

ORDOVICES

COMOVII

CATUVELLAUNI

ICENI

DEMETAE

SILURES

DOBUNNI

TRINOVANTES

DUROTRIGES

ATREBATES

CANTIACI

DUMNONII

English Channel

Boudicca of the Iceni

No written records were kept by the Iceni. This means that we do not know much about Boudicca's early life. She was probably born around AD 35. She married Prasutagus in AD 48. He was the leader of the Iceni. They had two daughters.

Villages in Boudicca's time had round houses with thatched roofs.

FACT

We know about Boudicca because of Roman writers Tacitus and Cassius Dio. However, they only give the Roman viewpoint and they wrote some time after the actual events.

Tacitus

Invasion

The Romans had **conquered** many countries by the 1st century AD. They successfully **invaded** Britain in AD 43. Local tribal leaders were forced to pay money and follow Roman laws in order to keep control of their lands. The tribal leaders were called client kings.

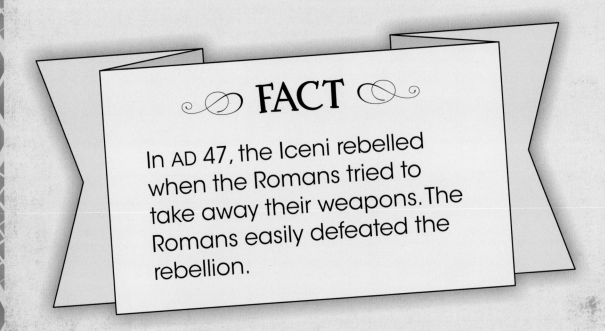

FACT

In AD 47, the Iceni rebelled when the Romans tried to take away their weapons. The Romans easily defeated the rebellion.

Emperor Claudius, leader of the Romans in AD 43

Change

In AD 58, the Roman **governor** of Britain died. Gaius Suetonius Paulinus became the new governor.

In AD 60, Prasutagus died. He left half of his property to his daughters and half to Roman Emperor Nero. This upset the Romans because Prasutagus was only a client king, not a king in his own right. He should have left everything to Rome.

Gaius Suetonius Paulinus

FACT

Emperor Nero had his own mother killed!

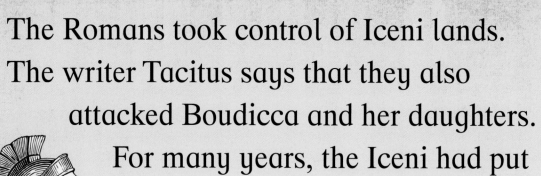

The Romans took control of Iceni lands. The writer Tacitus says that they also attacked Boudicca and her daughters. For many years, the Iceni had put up with the Romans taking their money and their weapons. They finally decided it was time to fight back.

FACT

Dio wrote that Emperor Claudius had given money to the Iceni for supporting the Romans. Catus Decianus was the Roman in charge of money in Britain. He demanded the money back. Boudicca was unable to pay.

Support for the rebellion

Colchester had been the capital city of the Trinovantes tribe. Then the Romans took over the city. They forced the Trinovantes to not only pay for a new **temple** but also to help build it. The Trinovantes were unhappy with how the Romans had treated them and willingly joined the Iceni's rebellion. Other tribes also joined.

This is a coin of the Trinovantes tribe.

FACT

The Trinovantes tribe was the first to be mentioned by a Roman author – the emperor Julius Caesar – in 54 BC.

Destruction

The angry tribes marched towards Colchester. Romans who were not able to escape hid in the unfinished temple. The tribes **besieged** the temple for two days. They finally got in through the temple's roof and killed everyone inside. Then they destroyed the city.

This modern statue of Boudicca is in Colchester.

❧ FACT ❧

About 10,000 people are thought to have died during the attack on Colchester.

The next target was London. It was a new town and not very well defended. Paulinus had been dealing with a rebellion in North Wales. He arrived in London before Boudicca but then left again. He decided that a **pitched battle** was the best way to beat the tribes. The tribes, meanwhile, destroyed London. Then they marched north, destroying another city, St Albans, on the way.

✺ FACT ✺

Tacitus wrote that 70,000 people were killed throughout the three towns of Colchester, London and St Albans.

The Battle of Watling Street

Nobody knows exactly where the final battle took place. The Romans were very experienced and disciplined. Boudicca and her warriors were unorganized, particularly as the army had grown in number. However hard they tried, they could not break through the Romans' front line of soldiers.

Boudicca rode her chariot, shouting words of encouragement to her warriors.

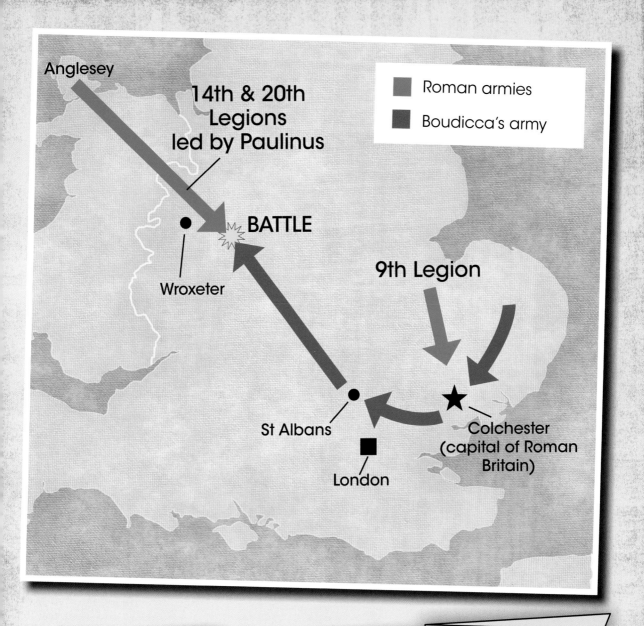

Anglesey

14th & 20th
Legions
led by Paulinus

BATTLE

Wroxeter

9th Legion

St Albans

London

Colchester
(capital of Roman
Britain)

Roman armies

Boudicca's army

❧ FACT ❧

There were about 10,000 Roman soldiers, but Boudicca's army was much bigger.

In the end, the Romans' **military** training helped them to win the battle. Afterwards, they killed everyone, including the women and children who had been watching. Boudicca died at the battle. Cassius Dio claims she died from illness. Tacitus suggests she poisoned herself so that she would not be taken prisoner by the Romans.

In modern times, people dress up as Celtic Britons and re-enact the battle.

FACT

After the battle, 7,000 more Roman soldiers came to Britain to help get the country under control again.

Legacy

Boudicca was a strong, powerful woman. She brought the often warring tribes of eastern England together. She inspired them to stand up to the Romans. The Romans were forced to improve their defences after nearly losing Britain. Boudicca and her rebellion had given the mighty Romans a big scare.

QUIDENHAM

❦ FACT ❦

Local stories say that Boudicca is buried on a tree-covered **mound** outside Quidenham in Norfolk. However, nobody really knows where she was buried.

Timeline

Boudicca lived many hundreds of years ago. At that time, people in Britain did not keep written records of what happened. This means that our knowledge of the time involves quite a lot of guesswork. The dates we have for Boudicca's life are not exact.

c. 35 Boudicca is born into the Iceni tribe in East Anglia

43 Roman Emperor Claudius invades and conquers southern Britain

c. 48 Boudicca marries Prasutagus, King of the Iceni

58 Gaius Suetonius Paulinus is made governor of Britain

60 Prasutagus dies; the Romans decide they want the Iceni's lands; Boudicca and her daughters are attacked

c. 60-61 Boudicca **unites** the tribes of the east and south of England against the Romans; Boudicca and her army destroys the cities of Colchester, London and St Albans

61 Boudicca meets Gaius Suetonius Paulinus in battle; the tribes are defeated and Boudicca dies

Note: "c." means the exact date is not known.

Glossary

besiege surround a city or building to cut off supplies and force those inside to surrender

conquer defeat and take control of an enemy

governor person chosen to be the head of government of a state

invade send an army into a country in order to take over that country

military relating to the armed forces of a country

mound small hill

pitched battle large battle fought in one place

rebellion armed fight against a government or group in charge

Romans people who came from Rome, Italy. They had conquered many countries before reaching Britain in AD 43.

temple building used for worship

tribe group of people who share the same language and way of life

unite bring together

Find out more

Books
Boudica, Claire Llewellyn (Collins, 2016)

Boudica and the Celts (History Starting Points), David Gill (Franklin Watts, 2016)

Everyday Life (Discover the Celts and the Iron Age), Moira Butterfield (Franklin Watts, 2016)

Iron Age (Britain in the Past), Moira Butterfield (Franklin Watts, 2015)

Roman Britain (Fact Cat), Izzi Howell (Wayland, 2015)

Websites
www.bbc.co.uk/education/clips/z8bg9j6
Find out more about Boudicca's attack on Colchester.

www.dkfindout.com/uk/history/celts/boudicca
Learn about the Celts' way of life on this website.

Places to visit
Norwich Castle Museum
Castle Hill, Norwich NR1 3JU
Visit this museum to see the Boudica Gallery and Trail.

The Boudicca Way
You could try walking some of the Boudicca Way path in Norfolk. It includes a Roman town, Caistor St Edmund.
www.boudiccaway.co.uk

Index